SURVIVOR

STEVEN CALLAHAN

Adrift at Sea

Holly Cefrey

Children's Press®
A Division of Scholastic Inc.
New York / Toronto / London / Auckland / Sydney
Mexico City / New Delhi / Hong Kong
Danbury, Connecticut

Book Design: Christopher Logan
Contributing Editor: Jennifer Silate

Photo Credits: Cover, pp. 11, 22, 32, 40 © Benjamin Mendlowitz;
p. 4 © John Lund/Getty Images; p. 8 William A. Ashbolt © 1965 The
Plain Dealer. All rights reserved. Reprinted with permission;
p.15 © Jason Hawkes/Corbis; p. 16 © Marcel Mochet/AFP; p. 20 © James
L. Amos/Corbis; p. 24 © Horace Bristol/Corbis; p. 29 © David Hall/Getty
Images; p. 30 © Joel W. Rogers/Corbis; p. 34 © Corbis; p. 36 © Digital
Stock; p. 39 © Pat Wellenbach/AP/Wide World Photo

Library of Congress Cataloging-in-Publication Data

Cefrey, Holly.
    Steven Callahan : adrift at sea / Holly Cefrey.
    p. cm.—(Survivor)
    Summary: Introduces the sailing enthusiast and boat designer, Steven
Callahan, who struggled to survive after his small sailboat, the
Napoleon Solo, sank into the Atlantic Ocean.
    ISBN 0-516-24330-6 (lib. bdg.)—ISBN 0-516-27868-1 (pbk.)
    1. Callahan, Steven—Juvenile literature. 2. *Napoleon Solo*
(Yacht)—Juvenile literature. 3. Survival after airplane accidents,
shipwrecks, etc.—Juvenile literature. 4. North Atlantic
Ocean—Juvenile literature. [1. Callahan, Steven. 2. *Napoleon Solo*
(Yacht) 3. Sailing. 4. Survival. 5. Shipwrecks.] I. Title. II. Series.

G530.C24C44 2003
910'.9163'1—dc21

                                            2003000642

Contents

Even boats, such as this one, that are larger than the *Napoleon Solo* are no match for an angry sea.

Introduction

From her safe, warm bed in the United States, a mother wakes in a panic. She has dreamt that her son was struggling to keep his head above choppy, black water. He was desperately trying to get some air. His mother is scared, sweaty, and shaking. From that moment on, she waits anxiously to hear from her son, Steven.

Over a thousand miles away, Steven Callahan is clutching to life. He drifts alone on the Atlantic Ocean in his emergency life raft. About thirty days earlier, his sailboat—*Napoleon Solo*—sank into the deep waters of the Atlantic. His life raft is supposed to last for up to forty days on the ocean. The fortieth day is rapidly approaching, but there is no land in sight. Callahan wonders if he will survive.

Finally, there is hope. Callahan sees a passing ship. He quickly fires flares into the sky to signal his location to the ship. The ship doesn't notice him, though. He is very disappointed. Pain caused by hunger gnaws at Callahan. Stormy weather brings strong winds and rough waves

that threaten to flip over Callahan's little raft. Eerie-looking shapes swim beneath his raft. They are sharks.

Callahan faces hunger, thirst, and the threat of being eaten by sharks. He is all alone, a tiny dot on an ocean thousands of miles wide. Steven Callahan fights to survive. This is his story.

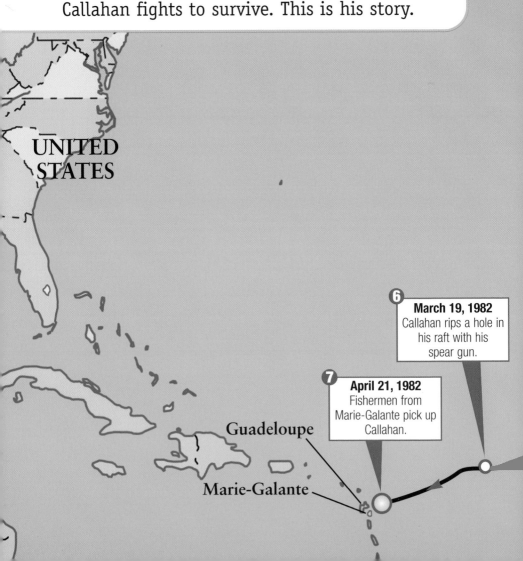

UNITED STATES

6
March 19, 1982
Callahan rips a hole in his raft with his spear gun.

7
April 21, 1982
Fishermen from Marie-Galante pick up Callahan.

Guadeloupe

Marie-Galante

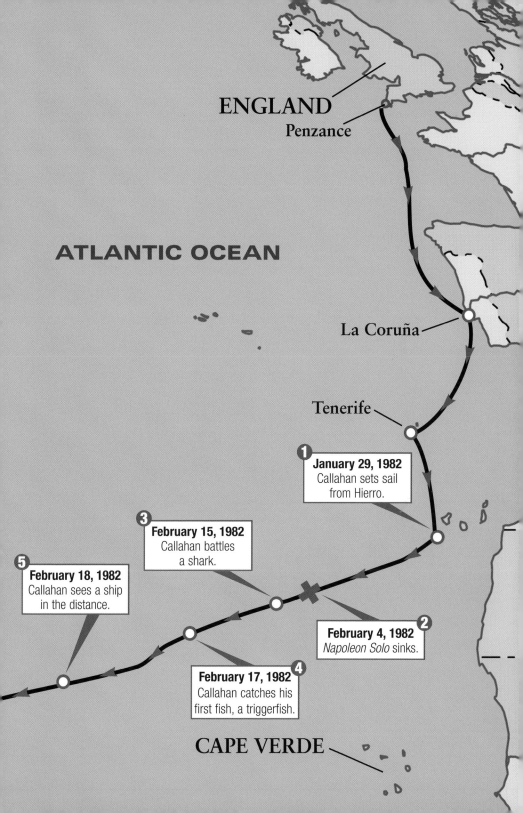

ENGLAND

Penzance

ATLANTIC OCEAN

La Coruña

Tenerife

1 January 29, 1982
Callahan sets sail
from Hierro.

3 February 15, 1982
Callahan battles
a shark.

5 February 18, 1982
Callahan sees a ship
in the distance.

2 February 4, 1982
Napoleon Solo sinks.

4 February 17, 1982
Callahan catches his
first fish, a triggerfish.

CAPE VERDE

Robert Manry's (in center boat) success as a sailor inspired a young Callahan to go on his own sailing adventures.

One

A Love of the Sea

As a child, Steven Callahan loved the outdoors. To satisfy his love of nature, Callahan was an active Boy Scout. He loved spending time in the wilderness. When he was twelve, Callahan found another passion—sailing. He loved sailing from his first experience.

Sailing offered Callahan excitement and adventure. He found the history of sailing interesting, too. Callahan read books about sailing and historic voyages. By doing so, he learned about the skills necessary for sailing and surviving at sea.

Sailing Heroes

One of Callahan's favorite sailing stories was about Robert Manry. In 1965, Manry sailed across the Atlantic Ocean from Falmouth, Massachusetts, to Falmouth, England. Manry sailed alone in a tiny boat called *Tinkerbelle*, which was only 13.5 feet (4.1 meters) long. No one thought that such a tiny boat could make the journey. However, Manry completed the trip in seventy-eight days. He wrote about his journey in his book, also called *Tinkerbelle*, which Callahan read with enthusiasm. Callahan liked Manry's story because it showed that even though sailing had been around for hundreds of years, new adventures could still be had. Callahan began to set sailing goals for himself. One goal was to sail across the Atlantic Ocean to England, just as Manry had done.

Boat Building

Callahan's love of boats and sailing grew as he got older. While in high school, Callahan helped build a 40-foot (12.1 m) boat. By his early twenties, he was living aboard a boat and working as a boat builder. In another few years, he was

Callahan did not mind all the hard work it takes to sail a boat. It was part of the adventure.

designing boats and teaching boat design full time. Callahan was living his dream.

In 1980, Callahan decided to build his dream boat. It would be the boat that would take him on his voyage across the Atlantic Ocean. He designed the sailboat to handle both light and heavy winds as well as powerful waves. It was a sloop, just over 21 feet (6.4 m) long. A sloop has one mast in its middle that can hold one or more sails. Callahan named his sailboat the *Napoleon Solo*.

Napoleon Solo Sets Sail

Callahan wanted to test *Napoleon Solo* before crossing the Atlantic Ocean. He and his friend, Chris, took the boat on a rough, 1,000-mile (1,609.3 kilometers) trip. They sailed from Annapolis, Maryland, to Massachusetts during the fall of 1980. At this time of year, gales are powerful. A gale is a strong wind. The gales tested *Napoleon Solo* and its ability to sail.

Callahan was very happy with his boat's performance on the trip. He felt that it was ready to cross the Atlantic. If *Napoleon Solo* made it safely to England, Callahan would continue his adventure. He would race in the Mini Transat. The Mini Transat is a race for small sailboats. Only one sailor is allowed per boat. The course for the Mini Transat went from Penzance, England, to the Canary Islands off the coast of northwest Africa. From there, it finished in Antigua, an island in the Caribbean Sea. After sailing the Mini Transat, Callahan planned to sail from Antigua back to New England. When he reached New England, Callahan would have sailed completely around the Atlantic Ocean.

Did You Know?

The deepest part of the Atlantic Ocean is 28,232 feet (8,695 m). It is 5,500 miles (8,800 km) wide and 9,000 miles (14,500 km) long.

Callahan and Chris began their journey across the Atlantic in the spring of 1981. They encountered animals such as whales and dolphins. They also faced more strong gales. Callahan loved every minute of it. He was finally having his own adventure. A dense fog greeted the men as they neared the coast of England. Nevertheless, Callahan and Chris safely docked *Napoleon Solo* in Penzance. Callahan felt a great sense of accomplishment: He had made it across the Atlantic! *Napoleon Solo* helped him to fulfill a life-long goal.

Callahan said good-bye to Chris once they got to England. Now it was up to him to sail his boat in the Mini Transat. He was excited about the trip and could not wait to get started on his new adventure.

While in Penzance, England, Callahan rested and got *Napoleon Solo* ready for the Mini Transat.

Many boats test their luck by racing in the
Mini Transat.

TWO

Going Solo

Gales swept through the English Channel before the race. The competitors were warned that the force of the gales would increase to "ten." A force-ten gale can cause huge waves to form, some as high as 40 feet (12.1 m). These waves can easily turn over boats.

Mini Transat

From the start, *Napoleon Solo* pulled ahead of the other boats. Soon Callahan's boat was sailing over 10-foot (3 m) waves. Callahan gripped his seat to keep from being tossed back and forth. He eventually adjusted to the rough sea.

Three nights after the race started, Callahan awoke to find water rising in his cabin. *Napoleon Solo* had a crack in its hull, the body of the boat. Callahan temporarily repaired the crack with some wood he had on board. He navigated the boat slowly toward the coast of Spain. Two days later, he safely docked in La Coruña, a town on the coast of Spain. Callahan had to drop out of the race. He was very disappointed about having to quit.

Callahan decided to continue his plan to sail to the Caribbean once his boat was repaired. Repairing the boat's hull took four weeks. Once the work was finished, Callahan set sail for the Canary Islands. A French woman, named Catherine, was on board to help Callahan. Together, Callahan and Catherine sailed to Tenerife, one of the Canary Islands.

At first, Callahan thought the trip to Tenerife would only take two weeks. However, there was little wind. Without any wind, *Napoleon Solo* moved slowly across the ocean. They didn't reach Tenerife for six weeks. Once in Tenerife, Callahan said good-bye to Catherine. He liked sailing alone and looked forward to his solo trip to the Caribbean.

From Tenerife, Callahan sailed to Hierro, another Canary Island. He stocked up on food and supplies for his voyage to the Caribbean. The Hierro locals were surprised that Callahan planned to sail such a small boat to the Caribbean, especially by himself. One person even called him a *tonto*, or fool.

Callahan wasn't worried about the trip. He loved being alone on the open ocean in *Napoleon Solo*. On the night of January 29, 1982, Callahan set sail for the Caribbean. As with the Tenerife trip, Callahan thought that this trip would only take two weeks. He also thought the sail would be calm. Winds on the ocean were not expected to be too strong. He had no way of knowing just how wrong he was.

Shattered Peace

The ocean was peaceful when the journey began. Callahan turned on the autopilot, which automatically navigated the boat on a course he had chosen. As *Napoleon Solo* sailed, Callahan passed the time by filming sunsets, drawing, writing, exercising, and reading.

On February 4, a gale swept across Callahan's course. The gale brought dark clouds. The peaceful quiet of the first six days was replaced by a thrashing storm. Still, Callahan sat safely at the helm, the wheel used to steer the boat. The helm was inside the cabin. He had built a Plexiglas hatch over the helm. The clear Plexiglas let him navigate while sheltering him from the wind and rain. He designed the boat so that he could do

many things while sitting at the helm. Callahan could read charts, steer the boat, and even cook a meal from his seat. Outside, the waves were growing over 10 feet (3 m) tall.

Callahan prepared for the storm. He checked his gear and made sure that everything was tied down. He also checked the hull to make sure that it was still holding strong. After the safety checks, he decided to get some rest.

Suddenly, a loud bang made Callahan jump from his bunk. Water rushed over him as he tried to understand what was happening. The front of the *Napoleon Solo* began to dive into the ocean. Callahan leaped into action. He hurried to get his emergency gear—and himself—out of the boat.

The water rose past Callahan's waist in less than 30 seconds. He struggled out onto the deck of the *Napoleon Solo*. Callahan inflated the 100-pound emergency life raft. A wave swept over the deck, knocking him and the inflated raft into the water. The *Napoleon Solo* began to sink as the waves

When a storm strikes, sailors must act quickly to guide their boats to safety.

tossed it about. Callahan was hundreds of miles from land, but he fought the urge to panic. The cold ocean water kept Callahan focused. He knew remaining calm could mean the difference between life and death.

Callahan's raft was connected to *Napoleon Solo* by a rope. He decided that he would cut the rope only when the boat was finally going down. Callahan had canned food and water on the raft.

He also had his knife and some emergency gear. The gear included solar stills, signal flares, and a pump to inflate the raft when it lost air. However, in order to survive, he needed more supplies from his sinking boat.

Callahan was wearing only a T-shirt. He needed more clothes and fabric for protection from the elements. He climbed back onto the boat. Inside, there were still pockets of trapped air. They helped part of the *Napoleon Solo* to stay afloat. Callahan cut some fabric off of a sail and grabbed a life preserver and a pole. From the cabin, he got a few important items: an emergency supply bag, a sleeping bag, and a cushion. He put the items on his raft as the boat began to roll onto its side. As more items floated out of the boat, Callahan grabbed them and took them on his raft. The life raft was tossed about in the sea. Callahan lay awake, not knowing if he would make it through the night.

Pounding waves and high winds can quickly sink a damaged boat.

Over the years, many people have been stranded on the ocean. They had only themselves to rely on for survival.

Three

Drifting

On February 5, the rope that kept the raft tied to *Napoleon Solo* was ripped loose by violent waves. Callahan could do nothing as he drifted away from his sinking boat. Soon, the *Napoleon Solo* was gone forever.

Callahan estimated that he was 450 miles (724.2 km) north of the closest land, the Cape Verde Islands. However, he could not make it to the islands because the winds and currents were moving in the opposite direction. The closest land he could drift to were the islands of the Caribbean, which were 2,071 miles (3,332.9 km) away. He would have to drift with the currents. Callahan thought that the winds and currents might carry him to the boat-traveling lanes, where ships sail to and from the United States. The lanes were 450 miles (724.2 km) away. If he could drift to them, there was a chance that he would be spotted and rescued. Unfortunately, that chance was very small since Callahan was in such a tiny raft. Callahan would have to find a way to stay alive until he was discovered or found land.

Living Adrift

The next day, February 6, was Callahan's thirtieth birthday. Originally, he had planned to make himself chocolate crepes to celebrate on *Napoleon Solo*. Instead, Callahan sat in his soaked life raft and ate a handful of soggy peanuts. He wondered if he would live to see his next birthday.

Food and water were Callahan's first concerns. He checked his supplies. He had canned beans and corned beef, peanuts, raisins, some cabbage, and eight pints of water. He thought that he had enough to last until February 22—if he ate and drank very little.

Callahan also had three solar stills on the raft. Solar stills are devices used to turn saltwater into fresh drinking water. Stills use heat from the sun to make salt evaporate. When the stills worked properly, Callahan could make about 20 ounces of drinking water each day. However, this amount was not enough to keep him going unless he had other sources of nutrition.

Callahan also had a speargun and some fishing equipment. With a little luck, he would be able to catch fish to increase his stock of food. Right now, though, there were no fish in sight.

Shark!

Callahan named his life raft *Rubber Ducky III*. He had owned two inflatable boats before and named them *Rubber Ducky* and *Rubber Ducky II*. As *Rubber Ducky III* drifted on the ocean, barnacles grew on its bottom. Soon, fish started to eat the barnacles. For days, Callahan tried to catch the fish, but was unsuccessful.

On February 15, eleven days since his boat sank, Callahan was resting in his life raft, dreaming of being rescued and going home. Suddenly, something crashed into him. *Rubber Ducky III* was thrown across the water. Callahan looked out and was shocked by what he saw. A shark was swimming beneath the raft. It, too, wanted to catch some fish.

The shark brushed up against the raft and bit at it. Callahan was frightened. He worried that the shark might decide that he would be a better catch than the fish. He was also scared that the shark's teeth or rough skin might tear his precious raft. If that happened, Callahan would surely be the shark's next meal.

Callahan started shouting at the shark and grabbed his speargun. When the shark was in sight, he stabbed it with the speargun. The shark's skin was so tough that the speargun just bounced off. Luckily, the shark became annoyed and swam off. Callahan collapsed in his raft. The shark was gone for now. Yet Callahan knew that it was only a matter of time before more sharks appeared.

Did You Know?

Callahan encountered about twelve sharks while he was adrift on the ocean.

The Catch of the Day

On February 17, a couple of triggerfish swam near *Rubber Ducky III*. Callahan perched on the edge of the raft and fired his speargun—success! He finally caught a fish. The meat of a triggerfish is bitter, but Callahan enjoyed it nevertheless. He ate everything the fish had to offer.

The triggerfish's skin is so tough that Callahan used most of the little energy he had to cut it open.

The fish's eyes and organs were the most prized parts for Callahan. They gave him much needed vitamins and moisture. What Callahan didn't eat immediately, he hung up to dry. The dried fish lasted for weeks.

Ship Ahoy!

The night after Callahan caught his first fish, he saw some lights on the horizon. It was a ship! Callahan fired a flare. Orange light filled the sky. The ship was coming closer. Did the men on board see the flare? Callahan screamed and hollered. He fired another flare, then another.

Callahan had made it to the boat-traveling lanes. However, his raft was so small that the ships could not see him.

The ship was coming! Excitedly, Callahan gulped down some water and fired three more flares. To his dismay, the ship's lights were slowly beginning to dim. He had not been seen. The ship disappeared completely. Callahan was alone again. He had wasted precious supplies for nothing.

Bottoms Up

Over the following weeks, Callahan was able to catch several triggerfish, some flying fish, and almost ten dorados. Dorados are large, very strong fish. As Callahan grew weaker, it took more energy to catch these fish. On March 19, forty-three days since being set adrift, Callahan wrestled with a large dorado and ripped a hole in the bottom of the raft with his spear gun. Callahan hurried to repair the hole as the air sputtered out of the bottom of the raft. He tried several different patches and pumped furiously to keep the raft inflated—nothing worked. In three days, Callahan was almost hip-deep in water.

Only the sides and top of the raft were keeping him afloat. Finally, nine days after his fight with the dorado, Callahan created a patch using rope, a fork handle, and other supplies that kept air in the raft for 12 hours at a time. He would survive another day.

Success! The patch that Callahan made for his raft lasted for the rest of his journey.

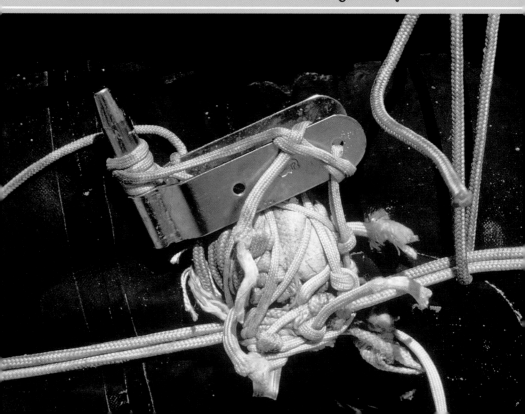

Winging It

Eventually frigates, terns, and other birds began circling around Callahan's raft. The birds came for the fish feeding on the barnacles beneath the raft. On his sixty-fifth day at sea, Callahan reached up and caught a bird that had perched on his raft. He ate the bird raw.

Land Ho!

As the days wore on, Callahan grew weaker and weaker. All of his solar stills were broken. Callahan made a makeshift water collector with parts of the broken stills. He intended to catch rainwater in it, but there was no rain. On the evening of April 20, 1982, Callahan looked out into the darkness of the night. To his surprise, he saw a faint glow of light. Was it from land? He pinched himself. Was he dreaming? No, the flash of a lighthouse proved to Callahan that he wasn't imagining it. After seventy-five days of being adrift, Callahan could see land!

Callahan had to be careful. Many of the islands near Guadaloupe have rocky shores that could have been disastrous for him and his raft.

Four

Safe Landing

The next day, Callahan was overwhelmed by the green color of the land. It was only about 10 miles (16 km) away. He was looking at one of Guadeloupe's islands named Marie-Galante. He had made it to the Caribbean islands.

Callahan wasn't safe yet. Reaching the shore would be dangerous. Ocean waves could throw *Rubber Ducky III* onto the sharp rocks or coral reefs. Callahan had to reach the shore, but he was too weak to swim or climb rocks.

Gone Fishing

At the same time, three fishermen from Marie-Galante saw the birds that were flying over *Rubber Ducky III*. Normally, these fishermen did not fish in that area. They saw the birds and wondered if that meant the presence of fish.

Birds were a welcome sight for Callahan.
They helped him survive and get rescued.

The fishermen, Jules and Jean-Louise Paquet and Paulinus Williams, decided to head for the birds. As the men approached, they saw what they thought was a barrel bobbing in the sea. As they got closer, they realized that it was really a man in a tiny raft. That man was the overjoyed Steven Callahan.

When they reached Callahan, the fishermen learned about his amazing journey. When he found out his rescuers were fishermen, Callahan insisted that they continue to fish instead of taking him to shore right away. They agreed and gave him some coconut candy. While Callahan stayed in *Rubber Ducky III*, the men went fishing. When they finished, they gathered Callahan and *Rubber Ducky III* onto their boat, the *Clemence*. They took him to the town of Saint Louis on the western coast of Marie-Galante.

Sea Legs

When they reached the shore, Callahan tried to get off the boat by himself. However, he was too weak to walk. He fell face down into the sand. Villagers carried Callahan to a nearby chair. Soon a van came to take him to a hospital. Callahan was treated for dehydration and starvation. He had lost 44 pounds (19.9 kg).

On April 23, Callahan's parents arrived in Marie-Galante from Boston. They were overjoyed to see their son. For months, they lived in fear that their son had died at sea. Callahan stayed in Marie-Galante for ten days while getting stronger. His parents wanted to fly him home so that they could help him recover, but Callahan did not want to be a patient any longer. He felt well enough to be on his own again. He got a boat ride to Guadeloupe, another island in the Caribbean. He did not want his adventures to end. His terrifying experience couldn't ruin his love for sailing the sea.

Where Is Callahan Now?

More than twenty years have passed since Callahan's ordeal. He still loves sailing and boat designing. Callahan recently used his expertise as a boat designer—and a sea survivor—to

Did You Know?

While Callahan never can be sure what caused Napoleon Solo *to sink,* he believes that it was struck by a whale.

design a new emergency life raft. It is called the *Clam*. The shortcomings of *Rubber Ducky III* were the inspiration for the *Clam*. It is the ideal raft that Callahan would have loved to have had on the last voyage of the *Napoleon Solo*. He believes

The *Clam* has a hard bottom and a tight cover to keep water out of it. Unlike the *Rubber Ducky III*, Callahan (shown below) believes the *Clam* is unsinkable.

it would have made the time he was adrift much shorter than seventy-six days. He hopes that the *Clam* might help others survive a similar experience.

Callahan's will to live helped him survive on the ocean in spite of the incredible odds. He had to overcome difficulties that some of us can only imagine. Steven Callahan's adventure is an inspiring story of survival.

Callahan was very grateful to (left to right) Jules Paquet, Jean-Louis Paquet, and Paulinus Williams, the men who fished him out of the sea.

TIMELINE

- **January 29, 1982** Steven Callahan leaves Hierro, a Canary Island, for the Caribbean.
- **February 4, 1982** The *Napoleon Solo*, Callahan's sailboat, sinks. After *Napoleon Solo* sinks, Steven Callahan is adrift on his emergency life raft. He must work constantly to fight hunger, thirst, and curious sharks that threaten his life. Whether he is learning how to fish or repairing a hole in his raft, Callahan figures out how to make do with limited supplies. He drifts about 2,071 miles (3,332.9 km)—for seventy-five days—until he finally sights land.
- **April 20, 1982** Callahan sees land for the first time in four months.
- **April 21, 1982** Three fishermen rescue Callahan and take him to the island of Marie-Galante.

barnacles (**bar**-nuh-kuhlz) small shellfish that attach themselves firmly to the sides of boats, rocks, and other shellfish

dehydration (de-**hye**-dray-shuhn) not having enough water in your body

dorado (**doh**-rah-doh) a saltwater fish that grows up to four feet long

evaporate (i-**vap**-uh-rate) when a liquid changes to a vapor or gas

gale (**gale**) a very strong wind

helm (**helm**) the wheel or handle used to steer a boat

hull (**huhl**) the frame or body of a boat or ship

mast (**mast**) a tall pole that stands on the deck of a boat or ship and supports its sails

navigate (**nav**-uh-gate) to travel in a ship, an aircraft, or other vehicle using maps, compasses, the stars, etc. to guide you

Plexiglas (**plek**-see-glas) a plastic sheet

sail (**sayl**) a large sheet of strong cloth, such as canvas, that makes a boat or ship move when it catches wind

sloop (**sloop**) a sailboat with one mast and sails that are set from front to back

solar stills (**soh**-lur **stilz**) devices used to change saltwater into fresh water

starvation (**starv**-ay-shuhn) the state of suffering or dying from lack of food

triggerfish (**tri**-gur-fish) a saltwater bony fish that grows up to one and a half feet long

FOR FURTHER READING

Alvord, Douglas. *Sarah's Boat: A Young Girl Learns the Art of Sailing*. Gardiner, Maine: Tilbury House Publishers, 2001.

Callahan, Steven. *Adrift—Seventy-six Days Lost at Sea*. New York: Houghton Mifflin Company, 1999.

McKay, Amy, comp. *Sailing Days: Stories and Poems about Sailors and the Sea*. Woodbridge, UK: Antique Collector's Club, 1998.

McNab, Chris. *Survive at Sea with the U.S. Navy Seals*. Broomall, PA: Mason Crest Publishers, 2002.

Neale, Jonathan. *Lost at Sea*. New York: Houghton Mifflin Company, 2002.

RESOURCES

Organizations

American Sailing Association
P.O. Box 12079
Marina del Rey, CA 90295
(310) 822-7171
Fax: (310) 822-4741
E-mail: info@american-sailing.com
www.american-sailing.com

National Oceanic & Atmospheric Administration
14th Street & Constitution Avenue, NW, Room 6217
Washington, DC 20230
www.noaa.gov

United States Naval Sailing Association
58 Bennion Road
Annapolis, MD 21402-5054
(410) 293-2130/2341
Fax: (410) 293-4845
www.navysailing.org

RESOURCES

Web Sites

National Oceanic & Atmospheric Administration (NOAA) Kid's and Teacher's Corner
www.yoto98.noaa.gov/kids.htm
Read about the ocean and animals that live there on this informative Web site.

The Official Sea Scouts Web Site
www.seascout.org
Find out about Sea Scouting on the official Sea Scouts Web site.

Savage Seas (part of a PBS series)
www.thirteen.org/savageseas/index.html
This Web site has lots of information about the many challenges sailors face in the ocean.

INDEX

INDEX

About the Author

Holly Cefrey is a freelance writer and researcher. She is a member of the Authors Guild and the Society of Children's Book Writers and Illustrators.